Pennsylvania

The Keystone State

Marcia Amidon Lusted

PowerKiDS press.

New York

For my son Sam, with love

Published in 2010 by The Rosen Publishing Group, Inc.
29 East 21st Street, New York, NY 10010

First Edition

Editor: Nicole Pristash
Book Design: Greg Tucker
Photo Researcher: Jessica Gerweck

Photo Credits: Cover © Kord.com/age fotostock; pp. 5, 11, 17, 22 (bird), 22 (flower), 22 (flags) Shutterstock.com; pp. 7 Rischgitz/Getty Images; p. 9 MPI/Getty Images; pp. 13, 22 (animal) © www.istockphoto.com/Paul Tessler; p. 15 © Jeff Greenberg/age fotostock; p. 19 Sylvain Granadam/Getty Images; p. 22 (tree) by Sue Day; p. 22 (Daniel Boone, Louisa May Alcott) Hulton Archive/Getty Images; p. 22 (Will Smith) Junko Kimura/Getty Images.

Library of Congress Cataloging-in-Publication Data

Lusted, Marcia Amidon.
  Pennsylvania : the Keystone State / Marcia Amidon Lusted. — 1st ed.
     p. cm. — (Our amazing states)
  Includes index.
  ISBN 978-1-4042-8124-0 (library binding) — ISBN 978-1-4358-3374-6 (pbk.) — ISBN 978-1-4358-3375-3 (6-pack)
  1. Pennsylvania—Juvenile literature. I. Title.
  F149.3.L87 2010
  974.8—dc22
                              2009007224

Manufactured in the United States of America

There is a state where horse-drawn **buggies** still travel the roads. This state also has the Liberty Bell, which is a famous American **symbol** of freedom. In which state can you find these things? You can find them in Pennsylvania!

Pennsylvania is in the eastern part of the United States. It is called the Keystone State because it sits in the center of what were the first 13 **colonies** in America. A keystone is the center stone that holds an **arch** together. Many people believe that during the **American Revolution**, people and events in Pennsylvania held the northern and southern colonies together.

This is Independence Hall, in Philadelphia. The Declaration of Independence, which declared the colonies' freedom from England, was adopted here on July 4, 1776.

Native American **tribes**, such as the Delaware and the Erie, lived in what is now Pennsylvania before the Europeans arrived. After the Swedes and the Dutch claimed the land, the English took over in 1664. In 1681, King Charles II gave the land to a man named William Penn. Penn called his new colony Pennsylvania.

Pennsylvania has played an important part in America's history. During the American Revolution, several battles took place in Pennsylvania. Then, the **Declaration of Independence** was written in Philadelphia in 1776. After the war, in 1787, Pennsylvania became the second state of the United States.

This painting shows the five writers of the Declaration of Independence giving a copy of the declaration to the Continental Congress. The Congress would later adopt it.

Pennsylvania not only played a part in America's making, but it also played an important part in keeping the country together. One of the bloodiest battles of the **Civil War** took place in Gettysburg, in southern Pennsylvania. This battle is what many people call the turning point of the war.

The Battle of Gettysburg took place from July 1 to July 3, 1863. One-third of the Confederate army was killed in Gettysburg in those three days, and they lost the battle to the North. After Gettysburg, the North began to win more battles, and it would go on to win the war. The United States soon became one country again.

During the Battle of Gettysburg, shown here, around 3,000 soldiers were killed.

Water and Weather

Pennsylvania is shaped like a rectangle. The upper left corner touches Lake Erie, one of the Great Lakes. Pennsylvania's lower right corner touches the Delaware River, where ships often sail to the Atlantic Ocean.

Pennsylvania has many rivers. In Pittsburgh, there are three rivers that meet in one place. They are the Allegheny, the Monongahela, and the Ohio rivers. Parts of the state also have mountains and rich land that is excellent for farming.

In Pennsylvania, summers are hot and wet, while winters are cold and snowy. The weather can change quickly when storms from Lake Erie or dry weather from the South move in.

Here you can see where the Allegheny River (left) and the Monongahela River (right) join to form the Ohio River (large river, bottom right) in downtown Pittsburgh.

Wildlife in Pennsylvania is plentiful. The state's woodlands have a lot of trees, including maple and birch. Colorful flowers in the area include rhododendrons and azaleas. The state flower is the star-shaped mountain laurel. The mountain laurel can be red, pink, or white.

Beavers, bobcats, black bears, and coyotes are all found in Pennsylvania. The state animal is the white-tailed deer. In the summer, white-tailed deer can be seen in fields and grasslands. In the winter, they generally stay in the forest to keep warm. These animals sometimes live near cities, too. White-tailed deer are often hunted to keep their number down.

Adult white-tailed deer have reddish brown coats in the summer. Their coats fade to a dull grayish brown color in the winter.

Pennsylvania produces many goods that are shipped across the country. The state is best known for making steel and mining coal. The H. J. Heinz Company, in Pittsburgh, is famous for its ketchup.

In 1903, candy maker Milton Hershey built a chocolate factory in a small town now named Hershey. Today, The Hershey Company is the largest maker of chocolate in North America. Many people go to Hershey to visit Hershey Park, a chocolate-themed **amusement park**.

Farmers in Pennsylvania grow more mushrooms than those in any other state. They also grow corn, hay, apples, and **tobacco**. Other farmers in the state raise cows, sheep, and chickens.

This is one of the many coal mines found throughout Pennsylvania. Coal is used to produce power, which is then used to produce heat and light.

Pennsylvania's capital city is Harrisburg, which was built on the shores of the Susquehanna River. Almost 50,000 people live there. Harrisburg is known for the many places visitors can hear music, see art, and learn about history. The city has jazz and **symphony** concerts and art shows. At the State **Museum** of Pennsylvania, you can learn even more about the Keystone State.

Another excellent place to visit in Pennsylvania is Philadelphia. It is the largest city in the state. One of Philadelphia's most popular places to see is Independence National Historic Park, in the Center City neighborhood. Many historic sites, such as Independence Hall and the Liberty Bell Center, are found there.

Harrisburg, shown here, was named after John Harris. Harris was an Englishman who set up a trading post in the area in the early 1700s.

Visiting the Pennsylvania Dutch area in the southeastern part of the state is like taking a trip back in time. This area is home to people who are members of the Amish churches. Members of these churches believe in living simply. They do not use **electricity** or telephones in their houses. The Amish use horses and buggies to travel instead of cars.

Because of the simple way they live, people are interested in these groups. Many visitors come to the Pennsylvania Dutch area to see these families in their buggies and their plain clothes. To visitors, it is like seeing how people in America lived more than a hundred years ago.

Most Amish people use horses and buggies to travel instead of cars. They believe that owning cars would lead to inequality among members of their community.

Whether you want to ride a roller coaster at Hershey Park or see an Amish buggy on the road, Pennsylvania is a great place to visit. Kids can go to the Crayola Factory, in Easton, where they can learn how crayons and markers are made.

Visitors who are interested in history can visit the Liberty Bell, in Philadelphia. Some people believe that this bell was rung to gather people for the first reading of the Declaration of Independence.

Those who like the outdoors can enjoy the natural beauty of the state while hiking, swimming, and fishing. No matter what you like to do, Pennsylvania has something for you!

American Revolution (uh-MER-uh-ken reh-vuh-LOO-shun) Battles that soldiers from the colonies fought against Britain for freedom, from 1775 to 1783.

amusement park (uh-MYOOZ-ment PAHRK) A place where people pay to go on rides.

arch (AHRCH) A frame that curves at the top and makes an opening, such as a window or a door.

buggies (BUH-geez) Small, wheeled objects pulled by horses.

Civil War (SIH-vul WOR) The war fought between the Northern and the Southern states of America from 1861 to 1865.

colonies (KAH-luh-neez) New places where people move that are still ruled by the leaders of the country from which they came.

Declaration of Independence (deh-kluh-RAY-shun UV in-duh-PEN-dints) An official announcement adopted on July 4, 1776, in which American colonists stated they were free of British rule.

electricity (ih-lek-TRIH-suh-tee) Power that produces light, heat, or movement.

museum (myoo-ZEE-um) A place where art or historical pieces are safely kept for people to see.

symbol (SIM-bul) An object or a picture that stands for something else.

symphony (SIM-fuh-nee) Long musical pieces written for a group of musicians to play.

tobacco (tuh-BA-koh) A plant used for smoking or other uses.

tribes (TRYBZ) Groups of people who share the same way of life, language, and relatives.

Pennsylvania State Symbols

State Tree
Eastern
Hemlock

State Animal
White-Tailed
Deer

State Flag

State Bird
Ruffed Grouse

State Flower
Mountain Laurel

State Seal

Famous People from Pennsylvania

Daniel Boone
(1734– 1820)
Born in Berks
County, PA
Pioneer

Louisa May Alcott
(1832–1888)
Born in Germantown, PA
Writer

Will Smith
(1968–)
Born in Philadelphia, PA
Actor/Rapper

Pennsylvania State Map

Lake Erie

Erie

Allegheny Reservoir

Allegheny National Forest

Scranton

Pocono Mountains

Williamsport

Susquehanna River

Allegheny Mountains

Allentown

Delaware River

Allegheny River

Hershey

Harrisburg ✪

Philadelphia

Ohio River

Pittsburgh

Raystown Lake

Monongahela River

Gettysburg

Legend

○ Major City

✪ Capital

〜 River

Pennsylvania State Facts

Population: About 12,281,054

Area: 45,333 square miles (117,412 sq km)

Motto: "Virtue, liberty, independence"

Song: "Pennsylvania," words and music by Eddie Khoury and Ronnie Bonner

Web Sites

Due to the changing nature of Internet links, PowerKids Press has developed an online list of Web sites related to the subject of this book. This site is updated regularly. Please use this link to access the list:

www.powerkidslinks.com/amst/pa/